Monster Truck Racing

Scott D. Johnston

Capstone Press

MINNEAPOLIS

Printed in the United States of America.

Capstone Press • 2440 Fernbrook Lane • Minneapolis, MN 55447

Editorial Director   John Coughlan
Managing Editor   John Martin
Copy Editor   Theresa Early
Editorial Assistant   Michelle Wood

Library of Congress Cataloging-in-Publication Data

Johnston, Scott D., 1954-
    Monster truck racing / Scott D. Johnston.
        p. cm.--(Motorsports)
    Includes bibliographical references and index.
    ISBN 1-56065-204-7 (lib. bdg.)
    1. Truck racing--Juvenile literature. [Truck racing.
2. Monster Trucks. 3. Trucks.]   I. Title. II. Series.
GV1034.996.J64   1994
796.7' 1--dc20   93-44566
                                          CIP
                                          AC

ISBN: 1-56065-204-7

99 98 97 96 95 94   8 7 6 5 4 3 2 1

Table of Contents

Driver Gene
Patterson has the
Bigfoot 10 race truck
flying high during a
monster truck race
in Lima, Ohio.

Chapter 1

Airborne Monsters

The official stands at the starting line surrounded by the giant monster trucks. The trucks shimmer in chrome. They are almost blinding with their candy-colored, clearcoat shine.

The **starter** motions. The drivers move the monsters forward until their front wheels reach the white line.

Red, green, and yellow lights are ready for the command to start the race. A starting gun would be drowned out by the thunderous roar of the motors.

When the trucks are in position, the official gives the "thumbs up."

Wildfoot driver Andy Brass knows from experience that this kind of landing often results in a rollover. This time he was lucky.

The mechanical demons breathe fire and roar to life. In an instant, the lights change from red to yellow to green, and they are off! The awesome force of the monsters is unleashed.

Horsepower explodes into action. The 10,000-pound (3,732-kilogram) giants blast forward off the starting line. They head for the ramps.

The first trucks launch smoothly. They fly high and sure. They land solidly, all four tires hitting the ground at once.

But the third launch goes crooked. The truck tilts out of control. It comes down hard on a front tire. Before thousands of horrified fans, it flips over and over, side over side.

Finally it barrels to a stop. The driver is shaken, but safe.

Next time—who knows? This driver might be the one who crosses the finish line first.

This is monster truck racing. Hundreds of millions of people watch it on TV. People have

spent $300 million to buy related toys, clothes, and souvenirs. Monster trucks are even in show business! A monster truck appeared in the movie *Roadhouse* and in a TV commercial.

Monster truck racing is the hottest new motor sport in the world today.

Bigfoot 11 rolls over cars in Salt Lake City, Utah.

Chapter 2

Monster Truck Beginnings

The first monster truck was a Ford pickup with **four-wheel drive** (or 4x4). Called Bigfoot, it was built by Bob Chandler. Bob and his wife Marilyn used Bigfoot to promote their business in St. Louis, Missouri.

Early monster trucks ran in **truck pulls**, **mud races**, and other off-road events. Then they began something new: car crushing. Fans loved it! Bigfoot crushed cars in huge stadiums. Thousands of screaming fans paid to watch.

Overkill flies over a row of cars.

Monster trucks now crush stacks of cars, buses, mobile homes, even other monster trucks.

Born to Race

In early races, trucks drove one at a time over obstacle courses of hills and junk cars. The truck with the fastest time over the course was the winner.

These races produced an honest winner each time. But they lacked the excitement and drama of real head-to-head, side-by-side racing.

In early 1988, TNT Motorsports unveiled the first monster truck racing national championship points series. For these events trucks would race side by side. The race was on!

Carolina Crusher

Chapter 3

Under the Hood

Three elements make a truck into a monster truck: its **chassis**, its **suspension**, and its horsepower.

The Chassis

The chassis is the frame that the parts are built on. The first monster trucks were built on the frames of pickup trucks. Later trucks were built on the frames of military vehicles.

The **tubular chassis** was created especially for racing. It's made from steel tubes welded together. These are stronger than older style frames. They are also easier to repair and maintain.

A tubular chassis truck without body panels

The Suspension

The suspension is attached to the tubular chassis. It is the system that smooths out a vehicle's ride as it goes over bumps and dips. A suspension might include **coil springs** and **shock absorbers**.

Most suspensions on racing monster trucks are built around huge shock absorbers. Some use springs or cantilevers.

The Engine

Engines for monster truck racing must be 575 cubic inches (6,145 cubic centimeters) or less. The trucks also have **superchargers.** They make the engine more powerful without making it bigger.

Horsepower is the unit of measure for engine power. Early monster trucks had 500 to 1,000 horsepower. Modern ones have up to 1,600 horsepower.

Bigfoot creator Bob Chandler works on a truck's suspension.

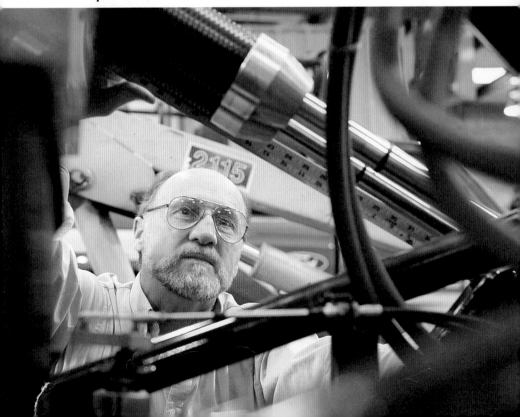

Mechanic Jay Diekman
works on a Safarifoot
truck.

Chapter 4

The Drivers
and the Crews

Monster truck racing is hard work.
Drivers are often, but not always, owners.
They usually have only one or two crew people
to help them. Together, they do all the
maintenance and repairs and build new, better
trucks.

Winning is hard even for the top trucks.
Andy Brass is a major league driver. He won
the 1992 Special Events Points Series by a

huge margin. Even so, he won just 6 of 17 events. That's how tough the competition is.

What It Takes

Drivers must have quick reactions at the starting line and during the run. A truck that leaves the starting line second usually crosses the finish line second.

It takes just seconds to bounce into a rollover. A driver doesn't have time to think. The driver must react almost by reflex.

Drivers must have courage. In every race they risk a pounding, the destruction of an expensive engine, or a rollover.

The Payoff

So why do they do it? Monster truck racers travel all over the world. Many have seen all 50 states in only two or three years. American monster trucks have performed in foreign countries, including Australia and Japan.

The drivers are independent. They don't have a boss telling them when to go to work and when to go home.

Snake Bite driver Ricky Rattler gets ready to launch his truck from the starting line.

Drivers never have to grow up. Veteran driver Ron Bachmann says, "You're still a big kid yourself. You never want to grow up. With a monster truck, you can do that."

Bigfoot 8 launches off an entrance ramp at the Bigfoot test track.

Chapter 5

Driving the Course

Trucks race on *straight line* or *oval* courses.

Straight line is a type of drag racing. Trucks race straight ahead and leap over one, two, or three sets of junk cars, hills, or a combination. Each race is 100 feet (30 meters) long.

Deciding the winner is easy. The first truck to clear the obstacles and cross the finish line is the winner.

Oval tracks also have hills and junk car obstacles. The track is usually 250 to 300 feet (76 to 91 meters) long. The trucks chase each

other around in a big circle. Drivers need more skill in oval racing than straight-track racing.

Getting Air

Dirt ramps lead on and off each set of junk

cars. The **entrance ramps** make the trucks actually fly, or **get air**. The **exit ramps** help smooth out the landings of the trucks.

Wildfoot and Andy Brass getting air.

Chapter 6

The Race

Drag racing is the most popular type of monster truck racing. The vehicles race in pairs. The winner of each pair races again against the winner of another pair.

Two surviving winners race against each other in a final round. Out of that round comes the champion.

The entrance ramps are the most important parts of the track. The steeper the ramp, and the faster the truck is going, the higher the truck will fly. The higher it flies, the harder it lands. Drivers call really steep ramps *elevator*

David Morris drives Equalizer.

ramps. They throw the trucks up really high, getting *radical air.*

An official, called the starter, **stages** the trucks. This means he makes sure they are evenly positioned on the starting line.

Christmas Tree

At the starting line is a set of red, yellow, and green lights for each lane. In drag racing, this is called a **Christmas tree**. The lights signal the drivers to go. They quickly flash from red to yellow to green.

When the drivers wait for the green light, they **torque up**. They hold the trucks in place by pushing on the brake pedal. At the same time, they speed up the engine by pushing on the gas pedal.

Scott Stevens and the Auto Value King Krunch race truck nearly roll over.

Dirt flies as Hercules comes down hard.

Then the light turns green. The drivers take their feet off the brakes and mash the gas pedals to the floor.

A driver must be sure to start the truck moving at just the right instant. If the truck moves before the green light, it is disqualified. Its day of racing is over. That is called **red lighting**.

Winning the Race

Torquing up and coming off the starting line is called the **hole shot.** The race can be won or lost with a good or bad hole shot.

The race also can be won or lost on the ramps and in the air. Drivers want to land smoothly, with all four tires at once, on the exit ramp. Many times, they aren't able to do this. Sometimes they miss an exit ramp completely.

Sometimes a truck lands at a sharp angle, with its front tires down and back tires in the air. Or it lands back tires first, with the front up high. Either of these might cause a forward rollover, when the truck flips end over end.

Sometimes a truck launches crookedly off the entrance ramp. It might twist while in the air and land pointed at an angle to the line of the track. This situation can cause a sideways rollover.

The worst landings happen when the truck comes down nose first on one tire. Then all of the force of landing hits that tire. That usually breaks an axle, which can also lead to a rollover.

Beating the Competition

The typical monster truck racing event has from 8 to 16 trucks competing. First is a **qualifying round**. Each truck runs the course to record a qualifying time. These times are

used to decide which trucks run against each other in the first round of racing.

From then on, the winners from each pair advance to the next round of racing. It continues until only one winner is left.

The racers compete for prize money, or the **purse**. The more rounds of racing they win, the more purse they earn. Purse is how the drivers get paid. It pays for truck repairs and for traveling from race to race.

Some races are part of a group of races, called a **points series**. In a points series race, drivers still earn purse for each round they win. But they also earn points—for each racing round, sometimes for qualifying, and for fastest time in the entire race.

These points add up. At the end of the series of races, the driver with the most points is crowned the champion of that racing series.

The roll cage can support Bigfoot's full weight. This protects the driver from harm during a rollover. After repairs, this truck went on to win the race the next day.

Chapter 7

Safe Driving

When monster trucks first started to race, Bigfoot creator Bob Chandler formed the Monster Truck Racing Association (**MTRA**). The MTRA goal was safety.

Racing means danger. MTRA makes monster trucks as safe as possible for both spectators and drivers.

Few people have been seriously hurt in a racing or car-crushing accident. Monster trucks are built with extra safety precautions to protect their drivers.

The radio-controlled "kill switch" (foreground) in the cab of the Snake Bite truck

Heavy steel **roll bars** are mounted above or behind the cab. The bars protect the cab and driver if the truck rolls over.

Special racing-style seats, lap belts, and shoulder harnesses protect drivers from bouncing up and down inside the truck.

Drivers also wear helmets that protect their heads, jaws, and cheeks.

Special fuel tanks and battery containers keep the chances of fire low. A special **kill switch** on the dashboard can be flipped if a fire does start. The switch shuts off the engine, which gets very hot during an event.

Following the Rules

Today, all monster truck racing **promoters** follow the rules developed by MTRA. A monster truck that has been inspected and certified by MTRA has met more than 100 safety requirements.

Almost every serious monster truck race driver has rolled a truck. Some have rolled over several times.

Since 1989, no driver using an MTRA-approved roll cage has been seriously injured in a rollover.

Glossary

chassis–a vehicle frame

Christmas tree–a set of red, yellow, and green lights used to start a race

coil springs–a spiral of rigid metal used in vehicle suspension

entrance ramp–a dirt ramp on a racing course used to launch a vehicle

exit ramp–a dirt ramp used to smooth out a vehicle's landing

four-wheel drive–also called 4x4 (four-by-four). Power goes to all four wheels.

getting air–how drivers refer to launching off the entrance ramps and flying through the air over junk cars

hole shot–the way a driver brings his truck off the starting line. Many races are won or lost because of a good or bad hole shot.

horsepower–a measure of the power an engine is producing

kill switch–a safety device that shuts down a vehicle's motor

MTRA–the Monster Truck Racing Association

mud race–a racing event in which specially prepared mud-racing vehicles compete

points series–a group of several racing events. Competitors earn points according to how they place in each event. The total points are tallied to determine a winner.

promoters–the people or companies that put together, pay for, and profit from the races and points series

purse–the money paid to the competitors in a race

qualifying round–the first round of racing. It determines the racing order.

red lighting–the lighting of the red light in a Christmas tree, which signals that a truck has gone over the starting line before the green light came on

roll bars–strong bars that protect a driver in an accident

shock absorbers–tube-shaped pieces that absorb shock when a vehicle rides over bumps or lands

staging–the process of bringing a truck up to the starting line

supercharger–a powerful fan that blows fuel and air into the engine to increase power

suspension–a system of springs used to smooth a vehicle's ride

torque up–to speed up an engine before a race

truck pull–a motor sports event in which the vehicles pull a weighted "sled" down a clay track

tubular chassis–the chassis made of steel tubes for racing monster trucks

To Learn More

Read:

Atkinson, E.J. *Monster Vehicles*. Mankato, MN: Capstone Press, 1991.

Bushey, Jerry. *Monster Trucks and Other Giant Machines on Wheels*. Minneapolis: Carolrhoda Books, 1985.

Holder, Bill and Harry Dunn. *Monster Wheels*. New York: Sterling, 1990.

Johnston, Scott D. *The Original Monster Truck: Bigfoot*. Minneapolis: Capstone Press, 1994.

Sullivan, George. *Here Come the Monster Trucks*. New York: Cobblehill, 1989.

Write to:

Bigfoot 4x4, Inc.
6311 North Lindbergh Boulevard
St. Louis, MO 63042

Index

Photo Credits:
Scott Johnston: cover, pp. 4, 6, 8-9, 10, 18, 19, 14-15, 16,
18, 19, 20, 23, 25, 26-27, 28, 34, 36, 38; USHRA/John
Disher: pp. 12, 30, 31; USHRA: pp. 13, 32.